I0475006

Integrity
Character
Leadership
Proven Techniques to Help New Managers Become Successful Leaders

By

Glenn P Clinger III

With

Robert M Clinger II

Integrity, Character, Leadership
Proven Techniques to Help New Managers Become Successful
Leaders.
Copyright 2021
By Glenn P Clinger III with Robert M Clinger II

ISBN#978-1-4583-3050-5
Published by Lulu Publishing.

Any reproduction or use of this material without the express
written consent of the authors is strictly prohibited.

Table of Contents

Dedication Page

Dedicated to our parents and the family members we have lost. Without the influence and support of these people, our lives would surely have been different.

To my wife, Alicia, the best thing that ever happened to me.

Matthew 7:12

INTRODUCTION

by

Glenn P Clinger III

I grew up in a small town in West Virginia. My father, Glenn, was the operating partner of a Pepsi-Co franchise in my hometown for thirty-one years. My father spent his entire life with the single desire to be the best at what he did. He was born and raised in Western Pennsylvania to a poor family and knew that hard work was the only way to raise himself out of poverty. His first job was a paper route at seven years of age, and that led to a job at a local bakery at thirteen. He was confident, so it was no surprise when he asked to run the bread slicing machine. This was one of the highest paying jobs in the operation. Since this job was a bit more dangerous than others, they usually reserved it for older workers, but my father needed the money for his family, so he kept asking for the chance to prove himself. Finally, the manager told him he was too short to reach the machine and would have to wait until he got a little taller. Never willing to take no for an answer, he fashioned a box on which to stand and work. His persistence eventually landed him the job.

A few years later, when he became old enough to drive, he started working a route for Coca-Cola in Franklin, Pennsylvania, and in his early twenties, he became the youngest manager of one of their plants at that time. Shortly thereafter, he met my mother, Joan. They were married and a year later, my sister Cynthia was born, and a few years after that, my brother Robert arrived. Then, Coca Cola announced that the plant he was managing was going to be turned into a warehouse. My father knew he could never make the kind of money he wanted running a warehouse, so he struggled to decide how to keep his career moving forward. Then he heard there was a plant in Clarksburg, WV, that was about to go bankrupt. It was a Pepsi-Co franchise that had gone through seven managers and things had become so dire that the owner was willing to give a large stake of the business to anyone that could turn it around. After a bit of thought, my father decided to talk to the owners and was given the opportunity. He borrowed twenty dollars from his father-in-law and loaded his family up in their old car and made the five-hour ride south.

I will never forget my mother telling me she cried when she saw the operation. In a field of waist high grass sat two old trucks next to a Quonset hut that served as the main building. She always backed my father's decisions but turning this around looked to be impossible. The majority owners lived in another part of the state and had no interest in running the business. With this being the case, it was no surprise that my father's first order of business was to fire the current manager before he could get to work. For the next several years, he would work almost twenty hours a day. His routine started each day by running a route, then he would return to the plant to bottle the product for the next day and load the trucks. It was a tremendous struggle, but my father was a unique blend of personality and work ethic. With those skills and the support of my mother, he slowly built the business. Eventually, the business turned around and began to flourish. More employees were added, and profits started to roll in. He had done the impossible and saved the dying business.

By the time I was born, the business was established, and my father became more of a manager. As a child, I spent a great deal of time at the facility since it was about the only way to see him. He continued to work long hours and would spend any free time socializing with people in the community to build rapport. During these times, I would watch how he handled the day-to-day operations. His years of managing others had honed his natural talent, and I considered myself lucky to be a spectator to what I now realize was a daily management seminar. How he treated people was special and you could see how people responded to him. It is hard to explain, but there was a connection that he could establish with people that was almost instantaneous. It was not long before his reputation was recognized and when Al Steele became the CEO of PepsiCo, my father was asked to the national convention. He later told me a story of how he found himself sitting at the main table next to Steele's wife actress Joan Crawford, who was now heavily involved in the parent company. They became friends and I can remember Ms. Crawford calling the house when I was a child. His work had paid off, and he was now considered something of a golden boy in this fast-growing company.

My father made sure all of us started learning the business at an early age and I worked summers there in Junior High and High School. After graduation from High School, I was unsure of what I wanted to do with my career, so I started working there full-time. I spent five years there working and studying at a local college. The years passed and my father continued to grow and improve his business and eventually, my older brother Robert took over a leadership role, allowing my father to slow down a bit.

At the height of the success of the business, my father and the majority owner started to think about selling the business. Not because they wanted to, but because PepsiCo was applying pressure. Corporate wanted to acquire all the small independently owned operations to allow for better operational efficiency. It became apparent to me how serious the offers had become when my father summoned me to his office and told me to go and pick up the President of RKO Pictures at the local airport and bring him back to the plant. His company was interested in bidding on the operation. My father understood the decision and being the minority shareholder, he had no say. Selling sounded good on paper, but the idea weighed heavily on my father. His main worry was what would happen to his employees. These people had been loyal, and loyalty was something my father took seriously. Many of his employees had become like family. Our families had grown up together, and he had developed deep personal relationships with them. When I was a child, his employees would occasionally drive me to school, and one even taught me how to drive a five-speed manual truck. Besides his faith, family was the most important thing to my father, and he considered these employees family. So, my father asked for assurances from the company purchasing the business that his employees would get to keep their jobs. Despite these assurances, I think he knew that the only way to guarantee this was to keep the operation, so he lobbied for that.

Despite his lobbies to keep the business, it sold about a year later. For thirty-one years he had worked himself to death and that Quonset Hut and two trucks had grown into a beautiful facility. Once on the edge of bankruptcy, my father saw his life's work sell for more than any other plant of its size had sold for at that time. He left the operation while my brother and I remained to work for the new owners.

The company that had purchased the business wasted no time eliminating many of the jobs in the manufacturing section of the facility and that was devastating to my father. I admit the transition was difficult, but I stayed on for a short time and then decided to return to college as a full-time student. My brother Robert stayed for several years to help the new company transition into our market and worked in a management position.

Eventually, Robert moved to South Carolina and utilized his management skills there to help several businesses. I, on the other hand, enrolled at Florida Institute of Technology to study aviation. Melbourne, Florida, was a long way from West Virginia, but I would visit my father at his home occasionally and I could see he was struggling with depression. It was as if he had nothing for which to live. He enjoyed leading others and now that had been taken away. In his mind, the golden boy had outlived his usefulness, and I could sense his loss. He had become very wealthy overnight, but his success was short-lived as he grew ill after the sale and within three years, he died.

After his death, I took a semester off to help my mother before returning to school. That next semester was hard, but during that time, I took a class in logistics management with Professor McCreary. The professor was a retired Colonel that had worked in military logistics, and he was also my adviser. One day after class, he asked me to see him in his office. When I arrived, he gave me a book on intermodal logistics and urged me to consider logistics as a career. I was impressed since this was coming from a man with such a long career in the field. I was not sure what traits he saw in me that inspired him to encourage me, and I never thought much more about the conversation until later. What I did not realize at the time is that he had planted a seed that would change my life. After graduation, I worked a short time managing restaurants and then landed a management job with a transportation company. A few years later, I moved to a large apparel company where I worked in international shipping and project management.

The years passed, and I eventually earned a master's degree and several process improvement certifications, and I share that knowledge as a part-time adjunct college professor. Despite all my studies, nothing compared to the education that I got watching my father. The things that he taught me as a child stuck with me and it was later, as I started to try to emulate his management style, that I realized how supremely talented he was at managing others. Over the past eighteen years, I have written many fiction books, but this will be my first non-fiction work. I feel it is imperative to pass along the management style of what I feel is the best manager I ever met. Sure, during my twenty-five years in supply chain management, I have worked with several exceptionally good managers, but none as good as my father. Keep in mind that my father's management style was developed before books on the topic really became mainstream. It was something that came naturally to him and that's what makes it so amazing to me. It is my hope that you will be able to benefit from this short book and perhaps apply some of the techniques. I will do my best to incorporate real-world situations that will help you gain a better understanding as to how and why these things are important. I appreciate my brother Robert for helping with the content.

CHAPTER ONE

Leadership is a Privilege.

-If your actions inspire others to dream more, learn more, do more and become more, you are a leader.

– John Quincy Adams.

What kind of manager will you be? That is an important question to pose to yourself if you are going out into the workplace. During my career, I have seen many managers and watched how they lead the workers in their care. It is sad to say, but many fell short in several key areas. My baseline for leadership was something I established by watching my father. He ran a very successful business for decades, and besides being a fantastic manager, he was an exceptional leader. You see, there is a difference between a manager and a leader and while someone may be good at one, they may fail miserably at the other. If you think about it for a moment, then I believe you will agree that many managers are not good leaders. If that is the case, then what are the differences and, as your career progresses, how can you be the best in this new role?

As you begin your career, you will most likely start as an individual contributor position. You will be responsible for the job tasks assigned to you. In this role, you are making sure all of your work is done to the manager's satisfaction. During this critical time, make sure to look at your manager and take note of their leadership style. Are there things that they do that you feel they do well or poorly? As you study other managers, you will be able to design your own style of leadership. It is important to learn from the mistakes of others and improve on what they do. Let me give you some key things you may want to remember.

As an employee who is promoted to a supervisor or managerial position, you must understand your life is about to change. Most of the time, employees think their manager just sits in a cozy office thinking up things to make their job more difficult. The fact is, a manager's job is to improve the employee's job function and performance through innovative thinking and introduction of new ideas.

How does an employee's life change? When you are an employee, you develop relationships with other co-workers within the department or organization. You may go out to nightclubs, ball games, dinner, or just hang out together. You form a bond or friendship with these co-workers; however, once an employee is promoted, that new manager must realize the whole relationship dynamic changes. Now, the relationship must be friendly and respectful. Notice I said, FRIENDLY not FRIENDS. All your years of working and learning your craft have paid off and as the boss, you now must be capable of giving directives to employees as well as issuing disciplinary action up to and including termination. That's right, you may have to terminate someone that has been a good friend. While you can remain friends if you choose, you are now the manager. In order to effectively manage, you must be willing to distance yourself emotionally from co-workers.

Leadership is a privilege and with that comes great responsibility. As you move from the individual contributor role into management, you are moving from a player to being a coach. Think about that for a moment. It is one of the most basic of examples, but one that will make you realize the transition that needs to take place.

You are no longer a player, getting the accolades, but now it is about the team. No matter how large or small the group is that you may be leading, it is now about the success of the unit and how it can best be managed to accomplish the goals of the company.

One of your new tasks will be to recognize talent in your employees and develop those skills. Helping the employee grow in turn helps the unit. This group of employees is now judged as a unit and the success of the unit falls squarely on your shoulders. One great thing to remember as a leader is that you now get none of the credit, but all of the blame. When you have a good month, then you praise the team. If things go south and you have a bad month, then you take the credit for the poor performance. As a leader, you must shoulder the responsibility for the bad times, because that is your job. Finger-pointing and blaming your subordinates is not the sign of a strong leader, but a weak and insecure one. If you do that, then your group will lose faith in you.

Many times, if an employee loses faith in a manager, then they will just leave and go elsewhere to work. The company may never know why this great person chose to find other employment, but it all comes back to the leadership style of their past manager.

I think we can all agree that losing one employee can be tough, but what if you had a manager that was causing several or perhaps dozens of employees to look elsewhere for work? This type of mass exodus can take place over time and often be overlooked by executive leadership as normal attrition. How can you, as a new manager, become the leader that you truly want to become?

Some people are born leaders, and some are not. Every now and then a leader comes along that display's exceptional abilities. The question is, what does this leader do that can inspire others to follow? What qualities does this leader have those others do not? Why do some managers struggle with high turnover when others seem to have the same happy workers year in and year out? These are all questions that many managers ask themselves as they work to find ways to become better at managing others. The real question you must ask yourself is are you a manager or a leader because there is a difference. Many of the best leaders have a personal code or a set of principles that guide how they interact with others. Major Dick Winters, who earned the Distinguished Service Cross for his leadership on D-Day, looked at leadership in this way. He said, "Strive to be a leader of character, competence and courage." This principle guided Winters, who was an exceptional leader. If he could inspire a group of men to follow him into combat, then surely getting our workers to do their jobs should be a breeze. My personal code was always, "I will not lie, cheat or steal, and I will not tolerate anyone that does."

The sad truth is that these types of leaders are rare and while people can be taught to be good managers, there will always be those rare few that are outstanding leaders. Many of these great leaders' abilities are developed in childhood and manifest themselves when they are given the opportunity. As with any talent, many of these individuals never realize how truly gifted they are until others begin to recognize them. The question is why some people are good at leadership and others struggle with it.

When you look at many large corporations, they are loaded with workers eager to move up another rung on the ladder, but many of these same people have little regard for subordinates when they are given the opportunity to lead them. It is not really their fault since their whole career has been about moving up and meeting their own personal goals and they never really learned how to lead. It can leave the new manager demanding respect from subordinates, but many times it never happens. Why is that? The answer is simple in that respect must be earned. Earning employee respect ranks right up there with earning trust. Just as in any relationship, trust takes time. I believe the attitude you take towards leadership is what makes the difference. If you lose that trust, then it can be difficult to get back. If you always look at leadership as a privilege, then that mindset is reflected in the way you interact with others. My father looked at things this way and said, "Caring means getting to know your employees."

As with any relationship, one must develop rapport. Doing that can be easier said than done. Whether you are managing in a large corporation or a small business, it can be challenging. In many ways, it can be more difficult in larger companies where managers often do not see subordinates daily. When you look at smaller companies, in many instances' managers work side by side with subordinates daily. This daily interaction goes a long way towards developing rapport. It also makes a big difference in smaller businesses when the direct frontline manager can hire the employee. They immediately can get a read on that person's personality and determine whether they will be a good fit for the operation. This is not the case in larger operations where you can be assigned a new subordinate. This requires the manager to assess the abilities and personality of this new hire or transfer on the fly, and it is challenging. I have managed in both environments and can attest to the fact it can be more difficult at the larger operations. When you are thrust into this situation, it all comes down to being able to build a solid relationship with employees. I see developing rapport as a two-step process which involves giving respect and displaying gratitude.

Caring about the people that work for you can manifest itself in many ways. If you know the business, and you operate it with the intent of earning a profit, then the employee can see that this is an operation that may be worth their time. Let's face it, time is everyone's most valuable commodity. In all our lives, the one thing we have a limited amount of is time. We can buy items, but there is nothing we can do to get back an hour of our time when it has passed. A manager must look at the relationship from the employee's point of view. This employee is exchanging the most valuable commodity they have for a paycheck.

Many new managers must take time to get to know the employee and show them you care about the mission of the company. Forging these relationships with employees can build a bond that lasts years or in some cases decades. Being able to build this kind of loyalty is rare in today's work environment. Many of today's younger workers do not stay at jobs for more than a few years to move up. I believe many times workers leave out of boredom and lack of opportunity, but many leave due to poor leadership. How a new manager goes about fixing this attrition and getting the employee to want to stay for the long haul?

General Omar Bradley wrote, "A leader should possess human understanding and consideration for others. By these means, their leader will get maximum effort from each of them. He will also get loyalty."

It all starts from being able to see things from their perspective. It is also imperative to understand and show gratitude and respect. We have all worked with those hard-nosed managers that treat employees like dirt and demand respect. Many managers say, "I'm the boss and it's my way or the highway." I cannot count how many times I have heard that line. Will there be times when you have a troubled employee? Sure. Will there be times you must release an employee? Sure, that will happen too. But being that our most important asset as a manager are the people that help us get the work done, then the question becomes, how can we become better at this process? I feel it all comes down to respect.

RESPECT GIVEN = RESPECT RECEIVED

The problem can rest on how a new manager can get that respect. This process can all start with a name. People like to hear their name and one could assume that at some point, your number of subordinates may rise to a level where knowing everyone's name may seem impossible, but you must try. There is a lot in a name, and that is how it starts. Calling that employee by name or saying good morning and adding their name tells them you respect them enough to recognize them as a person. I have a flash for you. They already know you are the manager, so it is up to you to show them you care about them. I spent a short time as a restaurant manager after college and I can tell you it was one of the most demanding jobs out there. I believe everyone should spend some time working in this industry to really appreciate the hardworking people that serve us. The company where I worked was tight on payroll, so many of the workers were paid just around minimum wage or a little higher. If you want a real challenge, then manage workers in this environment. The field is traditionally one with high employee turnover and at one point, our manager turnover was four hundred percent annually. When I first started, it was at an already established restaurant and the hours were not too bad, but within six months, I was asked to open a new store in another state. Faced with this new adventure, I soon found myself working one hundred hours a week and the pace could be grueling. Surprisingly, I had little turnover in the areas I managed, and I believed it was because of one thing, gratitude. I would try to thank my workers each day for coming into work. When I needed something done, I would ask them and not tell them. Many times, I would say, "Hey can you do me a favor." Many hard-nosed managers may not agree with that concept, but it works. I showed respect, and it paid off.

My father used a great concept to establish a rapport that I believe bears noting. He taught me to remember at least one personal fact about each person in my charge. Perhaps they have a child in school or just had a new baby arrive. Maybe their wife is going back to college to earn a degree, or they have a hobby that is important to them. This may seem unimportant to you, but it is extremely important to them. Those things are a part of their life outside of work, so write them down or commit them to memory, then make it a point to stop and ask the employee about it. This little bit of concern on your part will help them feel more connected to you. The smile

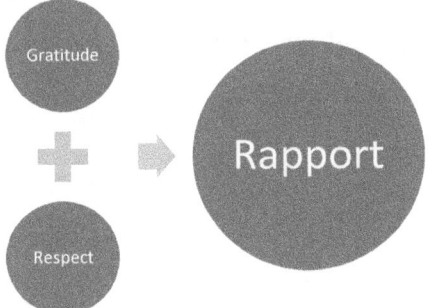

on an employee's face when you engage them in this way is priceless. I had many of them say, "I can't believe you remembered that." I feel a leader cares and that is what makes the difference. It is that caring that builds a cohesive unit.

LEADERSHIP

1. Leadership is a privilege, but that privilege comes with consequences.
2. Leadership is something to be desired by an employee.
3. Leadership is something to take pride in.
4. Leadership is the ability to make a difference within the organization.
5. Leadership is taking responsibility seriously.
6. Leadership is creating an elite workforce of employees who respect your position and authority.
7. Leadership is making a difference in people's lives.
8. Leadership is creating success for the organization through the employees you manage.

CHAPTER TWO

Everyone is Important.

-It is not about money. It is about the people you have, and how you have led.

-Steve Jobs

To be successful, employees must be molded into a group or team. Each person has a unique set of talents, and a leader will be able to recognize those talents and help them use them to their utmost. If you think of business in terms of being a sports team, then it becomes apparent that the key to success is finding the right player for each position. Imagine what would happen if a coach took a talented quarterback and placed them in another position. While the player may excel at that position, it is not the best use of the talent they possess. The same is true in business. One great way is to use the three-step approach, organize, deputize, and supervise.

The first step is to organize the work that needs to be done into manageable parts. Any process can be managed if it is broken down into manageable parts. Of course, some jobs will be more difficult than others and require employees with different skill sets. It is up to you to determine what employee best fits the role and then position them for success. Positioning them for success is the most important part of this task. You do not want to take a great employee and throw them into a job that does not suit them. All this will accomplish is to frustrate the employee and cause them to look for work elsewhere.

Once you think you determine the correct employees for each job, you deputize them. By doing this, the task will be theirs to do, and they will be accountable. It is then up to you to supervise the employees. The collective actions of many always produce greater results than the efforts of just one. In other words, having a solid team is the key to success. It is this process that can make or break an operation's success.

When you look at great leaders, they are always group oriented and recognize that someone acting on their own can be counterproductive to the process. The result of not instilling a team concept is that you eventually have individuals giving just enough effort to get their annual raise without an understanding of how their inefficiency impacts the company. Placing individual contributors on a team and holding the group accountable for results changes the dynamic. This creates a sense of comradery that can deepen the ties between workers. Many employees that have a substandard work ethic may try even harder knowing others are counting on them. Are you starting to see why a good leader is so important?

First and foremost, you must make everyone feel they are part of the process. I believe each person plays a key role in a business. The janitor is just as important as the CEO. I also believe that in many operations, the workers closer to the final customer are the most important. Some people call them customer facing roles. In a restaurant, for example, the server that talks to your customer, brings them their meal, and oversees their experience is the most important person in that establishment at that moment. That server is the face of the company. While the manager of the restaurant or the owner may feel differently, it still cannot take away from the impact that employee has on your business. If a customer has a good experience, they will probably mention it to a few friends or maybe no one at all. If they have a bad experience, you can rest assured they will probably tell ten people or more and you may end up with a bad rating online.

Many customers do not complain to a manager, they will just simply leave and never come back. At that point you have lost the opportunity to earn their long-term business. It can result in the business getting a certain stigma in the community. Here is a funny story about stigma.

Early in my career, I opened a restaurant in a small town in Virginia. When we opened the beautiful new restaurant, many of the people from the corporate office attended the ceremony. The people at corporate were always well dressed, and this was the case at our grand openings. For a while, our business was booming, but slowly our numbers began to drop off. Then one day, one of my employees mentioned hearing a rumor in town that the restaurant was owned by organized crime. Of course, this allegation was completely ridiculous, but I believe it began at the grand opening. In a relatively small town, men showing up in expensive suits and opening a genuinely nice restaurant must have fueled someone's highly active imagination. That just goes to show how rumors or word of mouth can harm a business.

That is why it is so important to have good employees in these customer facing positions. It is also your job to make sure they understand the important role they play in the operation's success.

When I was managing drivers in the transportation industry, I had one driver specifically that would always say, "I'm only a truck driver." I could tell that he felt his job was unimportant, when in fact, he had the most important job in the place. This driver always seemed depressed and somewhat angry. Perhaps he felt he had not accomplished much in life, but he was looking at it all wrong. Without the drivers, the business simply would not run, but he failed to recognize it. If he were not behind the wheel of that truck, the goods would never arrive.

I saw that a great deal in the transportation industry, it was something that contributed to the high turnover in many fleets. A lot of the drivers came to the transportation field because they wanted a job that allowed them to have a sense of freedom. Many of them had worked in offices or factories and now wanted something that allowed them to be outside travelling the open roads. When I would be given a new driver, I would always make it a point to find out what they did before they started driving a truck. It was fascinating to see quality control managers, office managers and even former airline pilots taking to the open roads.

Society has it all wrong when it comes to truck drivers. The people I managed in this industry were intelligent, hardworking people that would do anything for anybody. Maybe I am biased since my father drove a truck for years and I grew up around them when he was running his soft drink facility.

Don't get me wrong, driving a truck is a tough profession and requires someone with a unique skill set. Being a truckdriver requires the ability to endure long hours in isolation. At one point, we were switching from dispatching by phone to using only Qualcomm for communication. The unit in the truck was supposed to cut down on phone expense since all the dispatch and messaging was sent electronically to the truck. Dispatching by phone required you talk to most of your fleet drivers daily. When they made the transition to communicating only by Qualcomm, the driver turnover increased. I had one driver call me and say, "Glenn, you are the only person I talk to all day." It was heartbreaking to hear the disappointment in his voice. Despite the new rule, I continued to speak on the phone with my fleet drivers.

Turnover in the transportation industry is very high and is due mostly to the fact that it is very hard work. My fleets, on the other hand, had exceptionally low turnover and I never really understood why, until one day I called a West Coast terminal. I had a driver that had been sitting out there for several days waiting on some freight. I thought I would call and touch base with the West coast planner and get an idea of when a load may become available. Much to my surprise, one of the planners picked up the phone and began to berate me for calling. Apparently, he thought I was a driver interrupting his day. I stopped him in the middle of his tirade to inform him I was a manager on the East Coast. He apologized and confirmed my suspicions when he followed up by saying he thought I was a driver. That just amazed me, and I wondered why anyone would ever talk to another employee in that way. Then I realized why their turnover in that area was so high.

Not long after that, they had all of us take classes on how to get along with drivers. As I sat in these classes, I could hardly believe that this was so difficult for some of the planners. They had somehow gotten the mistaken impression that they were more important than the drivers and, therefore, had the right to treat them badly. It is imperative as a leader to let your people know how important they are every day.

Another thing that is important is to give them as much visibility as you can. What I am trying to say is that if something is going on in the company, and you can share the information, then let them know about it. Leaving people in the dark does not help anyone. Let me give you an example. When I was working at one operation, there were rumors that the fleet was going to be downsized. It does not take long in this environment for rumors to spread. Of course, this may be something they want to keep quiet to prevent drivers from looking for other jobs. Many of my drivers would come right out and ask me if I had heard anything. I would try to tell them as much as I could, but most of the time, I did not know any more than they did. I think my willingness to be a little more transparent was important and would calm them.

I would also make sure that they were knowledgeable about any processes or changes that may come down the line. If I had heard they were ordering new tractors or new equipment, then I would share as much as I could. I just felt that everyone has some skin in the game and trying to act like the gatekeeper of information was silly. The unit is the unit, and we must act as a unit with everybody working together for the greater good of the business.

My father always taught me to manage using the Golden rule. "Do on to others as you would have done to you." In other words, treat people as you would want to be treated. Managers need to put egos aside and realize that their job is no more important than anyone else. Everyone plays a role like cogs in a machine, and if one of those cogs fails to perform, the machine breaks. Each employee has a role to play, and everyone is important no matter what your title may be at the time.

CHAPTER THREE

Do Not Ask Others to Do Something You Would Not Do Yourself.

-If you are a leader, you lead the way. Not just on the easy one. You take the tough ones too.

-Major Dick Winters

First, always remember to lead from the front. As a team leader or manager, you must be willing to jump in and help when the need arises. Showing your employees that you are committed to the success of the unit is a key step in earning their respect. An employee is not going to give you respect because you have a manager title. Sure, they may acknowledge you as their supervisor, but true respect must be earned. Don't be the manager that sits at his desk and never leaves the office to visit workers on the floor. That type of behavior sends a message that you don't care and it can poison a department. Leading from the front also means getting to know the people in your department. By walking around and talking to your people, you let them know you are approachable. I have seen managers visit from a corporate office only to hide out in a conference room and summon subordinates to visit with them like a king calling his subjects. When they were done, they would leave without a word. It sends a message that you think you are too good to speak to them. I can tell you from experience that this crushes morale. Leadership is a people business and you must be prepared to talk to your employees and help deal with the issues that they face. If you have problems dealing with people, then you have no business being a manager.

One way for new managers to garner respect from subordinates is to be willing to work alongside them, to learn what they do. You may only spend a few days to get an overview, but you need to see what they do and how they do it. Sometimes it is the misconception of new managers that they simply oversee the work of others. Nothing can be further from the truth when it comes to leading.

When I got out of college and took the job in the restaurant industry, I knew nothing about it, so I went in with the mindset that I would learn as much as I could and do my best. I was in that industry for two years. I learned more about leading and working with people in those two years than ever before. I believe that time allowed me to hone my skills as a manager and that, in turn, allowed me to be successful later. One thing that this chain did during their training was require new managers to learn every job in the restaurant. In the span of the five weeks of training, I learned how to essentially run a restaurant by myself. At the time, I had no idea how important that would be to my success. There were many instances in that two-year time span when that training paid off. I was asked to open two new locations during my time with that company. When you open a new restaurant, you are thrust into a situation where many of the employees know nothing about the food service industry. That is why it was so imperative to be able to perform each job. It is amazing what people will do when they know you are willing to do it right beside them.

Opening a business is a challenge. Imagine being thrown into the mix with two hundred new employees who barely know anything about you. I can remember one Sunday afternoon the customers had been waiting out the door all day and there was not an empty seat in the place. As I stood on the floor talking to a customer, one of the workers from the dish room asked to talk to me. He informed me that the dish machine that washed all our dishes had quit, and everything was getting backed up. I told him to put soap and water, bleach water and regular water in the three sinks while I went and called the company to come out and repair our dish machine. He asked me in disbelief, "You expect me to wash all these dishes by hand?" I replied. "No, WE are going to wash all these dishes together." He looked at me for a long moment in complete amazement, then a large smile rode across his face. After I called the dish machine company, I informed my other managers that I would be spending the afternoon washing dishes. So, I rolled up my sleeves and stood and washed dishes alongside my two dishwashers. Despite the bad situation, we laughed and had a good time. The bond that I formed with those two workers that day was greater than you would imagine. I can remember when I was transferred to open another restaurant, those guys came and helped me move.

To lead, you must be able to connect, motivate, and inspire a sense of ownership. Heightening your capacity to lead others requires being able to see how you think and act and how your behavior affects others. Leading well requires a continuous journey of personal development. (Valcour, 2020)

Everyone has their own management style and having a more laid-back approach to managing is often beneficial. Micromanaging employees is probably the biggest mistake young managers make. It is a fear of losing control that pushes them towards this style of management. You must let managers or employees do the job you assigned to them and be there to help when needed. Micromanaging tells the department manager or employee you really don't think they know what they're doing.

Over time, resentment forms as the employee feels unappreciated. I've seen operations where the best people leave for no reason. You can look at exit surveys all day long, but most people will say nothing on those, and can you really blame them? What's the point? If management is supposed to learn from their mistakes, but they don't respect your opinion enough to listen when you're working there, then why would they care what you say in an exit survey? From my perspective, micromanaging an employee is almost like bullying them. When you see some ridiculous managers that require employees to list their time spent during the day on certain tasks, it just screams inefficiency.

When managers micromanage, they may:

- Take a controlling approach when completing tasks and projects.

- Walk around the office checking to see if employees are surfing the web or looking at their phones.

- Constantly check their teams online active statuses on Microsoft Teams or other online workplaces.

- Question the small details that are of little importance in a worker's performance.

- They often criticize a subordinate's approach to a project or the outcome.

- They often completely redo a team member's work even if the outcome was successful.

- Take away responsibilities without justification.

- Require employees to log every minute of their day and what they've accomplished.

- Require all correspondences and ideas be copied to them. (Miech, 2020)

You don't want to create a culture that says you're always right, and the employees are usually always wrong. So, invite employees to challenge your opinions. As they grow more comfortable in this role, they'll feel freer to discuss any performance concerns they have with you. (DuVernay, 2008)

By allowing your employees to make decisions, it helps to relieve the pressure and allows them to begin to feel comfortable in the process. During my career, I've met several key employees that had been micro-managed for so long they were scared to make decisions. This fear begins to impact their ability to be efficient. You're doing a great disservice to an employee by not allowing them to feel comfortable deciding. I can remember in one instance an employee had that problem and I pulled him in and discussed it with him. You should have seen the look on his face when I told him I wanted him to make the decision and no matter what it was, I would back him. If it was the wrong decision, then we'd fix it, but you must make the decision. When an employee has that freedom, their productivity increases dramatically. This is part of the mentoring process. By training an employee to make decisions effectively, you're strengthening the department and giving that person the confidence needed to grow in their job.

Once you give employees this freedom, you must also realize that sometimes they will make the wrong choice. If they do, never chastise employees in front of the group or team in which they work for making the wrong decision. If you want to run off all your good employees, then this is the approach to take. You hear it a million times as a new manager: praise in public, discipline in private. Any problems with an employee need to be addressed in an office with another manager present. Most important of all, remember to support their decision. Nothing is worse for an employee's confidence or morale than to override the decision they made.

I can remember working for a trucking company early in my career. My supervisor would have meetings every morning for about an hour, and he would ask me to plan the equipment that became available. Since I had been planning for several years in other fleets, it was a simple request. But soon I started to notice that many times loads would get changed after he returned from the meeting. There was nothing wrong with the loads that I put those specific drivers on. I was fair when I selected them based on the criterion which we used to make the decisions. But for some reason, he felt the need to overrule my decision. I can tell you when that happened, I never felt comfortable assigning trucks again. A manager that is unable to trust the subordinate should not be in that position.

CHAPTER FOUR

Take All the Blame and None of the Credit.

-It is amazing what you can accomplish if you do not care who gets the credit.

-Harry S. Truman

Everyone wants to be popular. One thing that you must do as a leader is allow your subordinates to excel. All of us have seen the managers that want all the glory and take extraordinarily little responsibility for anything that goes wrong. That approach is the easiest way to lose respect from your employees. You must allow them to get credit for things they do, or they will simply stop trying. I think it was Harry Truman that said, "The Buck Stops Here." That phrase can mean different things to different people, but to me it means when something goes wrong, then you are man enough to shoulder the burden of the mistake. It does not matter if you had your hands in it or not, you are in charge. Another thing that may be hard for new managers is to give credit where credit is due. There are times when managers may pass along an employee's work without giving the necessary credit. This does nothing to build camaraderie or morale. One-way to build good morale is to make sure everyone gets the proper credit. I encountered a manager during my career that was desperate to move up by impressing his supervisors. We used to call him the "gatekeeper" because he would always make sure we sent items to him to look over. He would then send them on to the corporate office. In this way, it would look like he was the creator of every great idea that happened to flow from the department. When that happens, you reach a point where people stop giving ideas, since they can see they will never be recognized for them. This may sound like a little thing, but it really does hurt the team. To build a solid team, people must feel like they can trust you to help them get the recognition they deserve. I will be totally honest with you and let you know that being in charge can be a lonely place. You must make sure the team gets the credit and if you are expecting gratitude, then you're in the wrong place.

You must be willing to be selfless and help your employees because it is just what you do. There are those rare individuals that like to do for others. Dale Carnegie, in his book, *How to Stop Worrying and Start Living*, had this to say, "If we want to find happiness, let's stop thinking about gratitude and ingratitude and give for the inner joy of giving." (Carnegie 127) That, my friends, is what I would call a leader. If you find any great entrepreneur or leader, you will find they have a deep sense of obligation to not only their employees, but to their communities as well. Look around at many of the successful businesspeople in your area and I think you will see this to be true.

When you are in a position of leadership, it is imperative that giving back becomes a priority. Not giving for the sake of being recognized but giving for the sake of giving. There are many people that are not as well off as you may be, so it is important to help whenever we can. That act of kindness is important and tells me so much about that person's character.

As we are placed in positions of authority, it is imperative to be able to provide constructive criticism. Always try to do this in a manner that frames the moment as a learning experience. One technique called the "sandwich approach" is often very successful. I would find a couple of things that the employee did well and sandwich something they needed to improve on in the middle. Here is an example.

Mike, I appreciate how you have been keeping up with the customers on your list. Can you make sure when you call on a customer to log it into the system? Overall, you are doing well, so keep up the good work.

You can make the point that he needs to improve on doing his customer logs in a positive way. That is a suggestion that may help.

For those of you that played sports growing up, especially football, then you probably will understand harsh criticism. Football coaches tend to tell it to you straight and often it can be difficult to hear. Once you get used to this type of unfiltered criticism, then you can absorb it and adjust. While it works, it can be hard to take. Years ago, they called the ability to take that type of criticism as being coachable.

During a practice session for the Green Bay Packers, things were not going well for Vince Lombardi's team. Lombardi singled out one big guard for his failure to "put out." It was a hot, muggy day when the coach called his guard aside and leveled his awesome vocal guns on him, as only Lombardi could. "Son, you are a lousy football player. You're not blocking, you're not tackling, you're not putting out. As a matter of fact, it's all over for you today.

Go take a shower." The big guard dropped his head and walked into the dressing room. Forty-five minutes later, when Lombardi walked in, he saw the big guard sitting in front of his locker and still wearing his uniform. His head was bowed, and he was sobbing quietly.

Vince Lombardi, ever the changeable but always the compassionate warrior, did something of an about face that was also typical of him. He walked over to his football player and put his arms around his shoulder. "Son," he said, "I told you the truth. You are a lousy football player. You're not blocking, you're not tackling, you're not putting out. However, in all fairness to you. I should have finished the story. Inside of you, son, there is a great football player and I'm going to stick by your side until the great football player inside of you has a chance to come out and assert himself." With these words, Jerry Kramer straightened up and felt a great deal better. As a matter of fact, he felt so much better he went on to become one of the all-time greats in football and was recently voted the all-time guard in the first 50 years of professional football. (Zig Zigler 112)

While Lombardi was a tough leader, he was able to recognize a time when he needed to reframe the statement that he made and use it as a teachable moment.

In today's work environment, there seems to be more employees that are sensitive and don't take well to managers being blunt with comments. People deep down want to be appreciated for what they do, and they want to get recognition for it, but there will be times when you need to be able to help that employee improve. How you approach each employee will be based on what you may feel will work for that person. The message must be tailored specifically to them.

Where many new leaders fail is in their ability to train. Often, the best leaders are good teachers and instructors. We've all been in that position of learning a new job and it always falls on someone to be able to teach us how to do the job. No matter what job that you undertake, there will always be some level of training required. Think back to when you took a new job. Do you remember the person that trained you how to do it? It's usually someone that has mastered the skill and can transfer the knowledge through communication. Contrary to what people think, not everyone can do that.

I have been in that position where you are constantly striving to gain some recognition. There are so many creative people out there that want to be able to make a difference. That is why being able to hire, train and mentor employees is very key to their success once they are working.

At one of my past employers, I was always the one that they would ask to train people moving into our department. One thing I learned as a manager is that everybody learns at a different pace. This is something that was valuable to me as I transitioned into a teaching role at a university. Everybody has a way in which they can absorb information. Some people learn by doing, some people can learn by listening. It is your job as a manager/leader to be able to instill that knowledge in your employee.

I can remember a specific time when a gentleman that worked in another department wanted to move up into our department and that required about six weeks of training. The person who was training him at that time spent about three weeks and did not feel that he was able to master the material. I can remember my supervisor expressing that to me. He then expressed how he felt this gentleman may not make it in the new role. When I heard that, I asked him if

I could take a crack at training him. I was not saying that I was better than the other trainer. It's just I have a different way of approaching the learning process. When I was in the restaurant industry, my supervisor told me that to be promoted you had to train the person who would take your job. One of the biggest compliments anyone ever paid me in that industry was when my boss told me he thought I could teach anybody anything. I believe that ability comes from the way I look at material and understand how that specific person learns. I always tell my students that if I cannot explain it to a third grader, then I don't understand it well enough myself.

So, the next day, I walked in and told this gentleman that I would now be training him. He looked dejected, as if the other trainer had given up. He hung his head and said, "Maybe I should just go back to my old job. I don't think I can learn this." He had been working at the company twenty-five plus years and in my mind, he'd earned the right to have that position if he wanted it. I told him that the process will take as long as it takes for you to learn it. I explained to him to watch me do the job for the next several days and take notes. Then do the job exactly as I performed it. Once he'd achieved the necessary repetitions, he could come up with his own system, but until then, he would be able to make it through the day and perform all the job functions.

Each week, I would spend less and less time with him. Just stopping by occasionally to see how he was doing was all he needed. It was obvious he was getting better at the job as he gained confidence. Then, one day, he made a big mistake that snowballed and impacted several different things. That is the thing about logistics, if you miss a detail, it can really impact the entire process. I'll never forget the look of panic that covered his face. He had reached a point of being overwhelmed. He did not have the depth of knowledge to deal with a problem of this magnitude. I smiled at him and asked him to move aside. It took me about thirty minutes to fix the issue and get everything running smoothly again.

In a matter of a few weeks, he was trained and in his new role. I don't think I was ever as proud of anybody as I was of him. He had hung in there and not given up and that says something. Some research shows that the most reliable predictor of true leadership is an individual's ability to find meaning in negative events and learn from even the most trying circumstances. (Thomas, 2002)

Based on the past twenty-five years of experience that this gentleman had in the industry there was no doubt in my mind that he could overcome any adversity, and that is why I was so determined to give him the opportunity.

As a leader, you must always be looking for opportunities to teach. Of course, great leaders don't limit themselves to teaching about work, but they also can provide deeper wisdom about life. The former CEO of Burger King Jeff Campbell said of the late Norman Brinker, a legend in the fast casual dining industry and one of Campbell's early bosses. "It's clear that he really cared about how guests felt and what kind of people he had working for him." Many exceptional leaders routinely spend time in the trenches with employees passing on technical skills, general tactics, business principles and life lessons. (Finkelstein, 2018)

CHAPTER FIVE

Always Set a Good Example.

-I speak to everyone in the same way, whether he is the garbage man or the president of the university.

-Albert Einstein

The way we treat others is important, especially in business. You must always hold yourself to a higher standard. My father always tried to be a principled leader. He had deep religious faith, and it was evident in the way he dealt with others. Do not get me wrong, he was a hard man, but he lived his life by following the ten commandments and The Golden Rule. Here is one example that has always stuck with me.

One day, a young boy was caught trying to steal some items from my father's facility. When the manager brought him in to speak to my father, he had every intention of turning him over to the police. The young man, probably 9 or 10 years old, was not very well dressed and obviously intimidated by the situation, and rightfully so. My father asked him, "You realize it's not right to steal, don't you?" The young man sat silent. My father studied him for a long moment before he asked him, "You know that stealing violates one of the ten commandments?" The young man continued to sit in silence before he responded in a low voice. "What are the ten commandments?"

My father sat back in his chair and was amazed. It was apparent the boy had not had the privilege of being brought up in a Christian home. After thinking about it for a few minutes, my father told the boy. "If you return in one week and recite the ten commandments to me, then I won't press charges." Anxious to leave the building, the boy accepted the offer and dashed out of the office. Assuming he would never see this young man again, my father thought nothing of it. He was quite shocked when the boy reappeared a week later and stood in his office and recited the ten commandments to him. Years later, this young man thanked my father. While this may not seem like much, I believe my father saw this as a teachable moment and it changed that young man's life. Sometimes all it takes is an act of kindness to change somebody's life forever. I believe that is why setting a good example is so important.

Think of how you look at the people you encounter each day. You may see someone walking around in an old flannel robe and bedroom slippers, but would you want that person to work as your financial planner or real estate agent? Whether you like it or not, people will judge you by the way you dress and the way you handle yourself. It is about setting a good example even when you think others are not watching. Let me share a story.

One summer when I was in high school, I went to football camp with my good friend Sam Holyfield and my younger brother, Matt. The football camp was it Slippery Rock College in Slippery Rock PA where my Uncle Doug had been the linebacker coach for several decades. It was no different from any other football camp, but one encounter impacted my life. Each day, the quarterbacks would break off to work with the position coach. The quarterback coach at the camp that year had been an All-American at Indiana University and one day he talked to us about setting an example. He said, "You ask any young boy in your neighborhood who the guard or tackle on the football team is and they probably will not know. If you ask them who the quarterback is, then I guarantee you they will know you. When you leave your home, go to school, or you go out with your friends, there are hundreds of little eyes watching you. Those young boys look up to you and they are going to imitate you and want to be like you. If you get in trouble, if you drink, if you smoke or are disrespectful, they will see it. So, remember that and always set a good example." I thought that was a great way of sharing that information and after that, I always tried my best to set a good example.

It also made me realize that how we treat others is so important. My former brother-in-law John Noland was a sportscaster in Honolulu, Hawaii. My sister was married to John for a short time and the marriage resulted in the birth of my niece, Alana. Over the years, we remained friends until John's tragic death in 2018. I remember one time when I was visiting them in Hawaii; I was talking to a gentleman on the beach who was in the military and set to head back to the mainland in a couple of days. We got talking about sports and he mentioned watching his favorite sportscaster on Channel Four named John Noland. He kept talking about John being his favorite on air personality. I found that to be interesting, so when John walked up from the beach, I made it a point to introduce him to these people. I will never forget how excited this man was to meet John, but what really impressed me was how John treated them. You would have thought these people were the most important people in town. John sat and talked to them for about an hour and even invited them to come to the studio for a tour before they left town. I thought that was a genuinely nice way to treat someone, and it was the way you would want to be treated if the roles were reversed.

You see, this does not apply just in business; it applies in your everyday life. I think that is what that coach was trying to tell me so many years ago. We set an example every day that others see, so do your best to make a good example that others would be proud to follow. Everything starts with appearance. Always dress for success and try to instill that mindset into your subordinates. It's the little details, that make a difference and being able to portray that to your employees is key. If you can teach your employees to manage the small details it will pay off down the road.

One of the best books ever written on increasing corporate performance was titled "Good To Great." In this book, the author, Jim Collins, talked about a culture of discipline in this way.

All companies have culture, some companies have discipline, but few companies have a culture of discipline. When you have disciplined people, you don't need hierarchy. When you have disciplined thought, you don't need bureaucracy. When you have disciplined action, you don't need excessive controls. When you combine a culture of discipline with an ethic of entrepreneurship, you get the magical alchemy of great performance. (Collins, 122)

Nothing is worse than to come into work walking on eggshells and not knowing what kind of mood your boss is going to be in that day. People like consistency. If you ask most people what they want out of life, they'll say to be happy. Sometimes we never know what makes some people happy and for each of us, the answer may be different. Take a minute and rate what you think is important, with 1 being the most important and 5 the least

_____ Money.

_____ Family.

_____ Love.

_____ Respect.

_____ Position.

There is no right or wrong answer with the exercise it just gives you a little better understanding of how you view work in the grand scheme of things.

What is important to you? Where do your priorities rest? You see achievers operate differently. They have an eye for the essential. They pause just long enough to decide what matters and then allow what matters to drive their day. Achievers do sooner what others plan to do later. (Keller, 35)

Discipline breeds consistency, and that helps improve operations. Under high stress, fast-paced crisis situations, a leader can never work at the level of perfection but having learned something about perfection as a routine not as a peak state, a leader can learn to quickly surmise what alternatives are available to assess his priorities and to make the most of time available. (Donnithorne, 36)

It is your job as a leader to see what matters to the people you manage. Knowing an employee's priorities will allow you to affectively motivate those subordinates. The point of the exercise earlier was to help you understand that motivation just isn't simply about giving someone an order. You must motivate them by convincing them that the objective to which you are striving to achieve on behalf of the company is in their best interests as well. In lower paying positions, workers will walk out and go to a new job for even a little more money per hour. Obviously, in their case, money was their prime motivation. This is not uncommon in lower wage positions. People must feed their families and to do that, they must make a living wage. But as a leader, you need to provide a work environment from which the employee does not want to leave. If they come into work every day, to a relatively stress-free job, where they can perform their duties while feeling appreciated, valued, and have a sense of belonging, that changes everything.

CHAPTER SIX

Managing Employees to Keep Them Productive.

-You manage things; you lead people.

-Rear Admiral Grace Hopper.

Management is a people business and being able to identify with your worker is the key. Try to remember what motivated you before your promotion to management and keep that in mind. The underlying issue is to find out what motivates each person and that is as different as the people that do the job.

Coming from working in a family-owned business, I had a sense of ownership instilled in me at a very early age. When something needed to be done, we had to make sure that it got done. I can remember one night when I was in junior high school, my father's warehouse workers on the night shift failed to show up. Knowing the trucks had to be loaded for the next day, he dispatched my brother to go and help. He instructed me to go along and try to get all the equipment loaded. I didn't really think anything about it because I knew it had to be done. When you are brought up in that type of environment, you look at productivity in a completely different way. When I had to decide on how to spend company money, I always looked at it from a return-on-investment perspective. That's what always made it so easy for me to do process improvement projects. My mind has always been geared towards finding a way to achieve the objective at the least possible expense. Many employees go to a job, never realizing the impact that they may have on the company. It is your job as a leader to give them that insight into the decision-making process and help them understand. Whether it is your business or not, saving money and improving processes can instill a sense of pride and accomplishment into an employee.

Another thing that is important is to be free with praise and compliments. Taking the time to compliment someone's work may only take a minute, but it can mean a great deal to your employee. Sometimes having an award that is given out each month to the team with the highest sales or lowest turnover can generate competition. Whatever you do, recognize the efforts, and set an example of excellence. Many times, all it takes is a simple compliment. Often competition can bring out the best and the worst in people, so keep things lighthearted and fun.

Remember, employees do not have to like each other, but they must work with one another. To use a sports analogy, imagine you're the owner of a Pro Football team and you want to win the Super Bowl. Athletes at that level realize this is a job and they are expected to perform. You don't have to like the people that work with you, but you must respect their abilities. For example, it doesn't matter if you're the guard, tackle, center, quarterback or running back, your job is to execute. The coach and players must leave their differences at the gate of the stadium and come in and play as a team to win. Players have disagreements all the time, fights in the locker room, or disagreements on the practice field, but game time requires them to put that aside and work together for a goal. Many times, the people you may think will never get along will end up being friends when placed in an environment where they have common goals and must work together.

Another example would be looking at state and local government. If you are the general manager of an operation, you could relate that position to being the Governor of a state or the President of the United States.

A general manager cannot run the company alone, likewise for the President or Governor. These government organizations are an extremely complex multilayered matrix of people with varying talents, abilities, and egos.

Let's assume that each one of your department managers represents a cabinet position. One department manager may be the Secretary of Transportation and one department manager, the Secretary of Defense. Each position has a responsibility to manage their department. Once you deputize these department managers, you must give them the freedom to do their jobs. Let the managers run their respective departments and if everyone does their job, the team wins and is successful.

In many instances, good employees become pigeonholed in jobs where they excel and are never, ever given a chance to move any higher. That is totally unfair for the employee and results in low morale and eventually high turnover.

In a perfect world, you could bring along your best people with you as you moved up the ladder, but I can tell you this rarely happens. Most of the time, as managers are promoted, they leave, never to be seen or heard from again. What does it say about you as a manager if you are promoted to a corporate level and an opportunity arises that would be a good fit for one of your past subordinates and you fail to recommend them? The operative word in that sentence is fail because you have failed in your responsibility to help the people that helped you. I have got news for you; you would not be in that new position without the people that worked for you. Remember, it all goes back to loyalty and loyalty is the key. There are a lot of things in life that people can be, but nothing is as valuable as somebody that is loyal to you. It is extremely hard to find trusting and loyal employees and that loyalty should be returned whenever possible.

You need to be nice to the people on the way up the ladder, because you will meet those same people on the way back down, and all of us come down. Remember, don't burn any bridges, and make sure you treat everyone as you would want to be treated.

Another aspect of being productive is motivation, and everybody is motivated by different things. We all like to make more money, but believe it or not, that is of little regard to some workers. But what really helps to motivate workers?

1. Recognition – I would have to say that taking the time to thank them is number one. It is amazing the impact a few kind words can do, especially in a group setting. If you oversee a team, perhaps recognize a specific employee each month for a job well done. At one place where I worked, they had this crummy little plastic trophy that was presented each month to the winning team. It was unbelievable how people would work to win that thing and to have bragging rights for a month.

2. Lunch outing – Take a different employee out to lunch each week. It is a way of thanking them and it also allows you to get to know them better. Many bosses take groups of employees to lunch and that's fine, but I feel that taking smaller groups or taking just one employee to lunch occasionally will allow them to openly discuss any ideas or problems freely.

3. Give them the credit – If someone does a good job, then make sure they get the credit. Make it a point to call out your star workers and help them to move their career along.

4. Throw company parties – Have a party every now and then to let them know you care. Nothing builds relationships like get togethers. Many times, employees will stay at jobs simply for the co-workers and manager they have at the time. Doing your best to make the office more like a family will lower turnover.

5. Make each employee part of the process – Let everyone know what is happening. If you are thinking about getting new software that impacts everyone, then mention it. No one ever likes to get something thrown on them at the last minute.

6. Let them feel some independence – Nothing squashes morale like a manager that is micromanaging the work. If you let employees have some breathing room, then you will be amazed at what they can accomplish.

Keeping employees productive and happy is the biggest juggling act in management. One-way employees can be more productive is to be physically healthy. When you feel better, physically, it shows in your work. My younger brother, Matt, is a successful personal trainer and has been for years. I had concerns about someone who was physically unfit and overweight, so I asked his advice. He summed it up this way, "For some people, beginning to exercise and take care of themselves physically is like finding religion. By the time they get around to doing it, the damage has already been done. It's a lifestyle change to stay physically fit." I cannot help but feel fitness is a key in lowering employee turnover.

How are some managers able to keep turnover low in fields that are primarily high turnover occupations? I experienced this firsthand in the transportation industry. Truck drivers are vital to the flow of the supply chain, yet this key resource is being drained at an alarming rate.

The average life expectancy for long-haul truck drivers is 61 years. As the current truck driver workforce ages and with fewer young people choosing a career as a truck driver, it leaves the industry with a major problem. How can these key individuals be replaced? Companies are scrambling to try initiatives such as sign-on and referral bonuses to lessen the impending shortage, but there is a better way.

Driving a truck for a living is a difficult job and those who choose it for a career find themselves enduring long stints away from family. They also end up not eating a balanced diet and many get little exercise while spending most of their day behind the wheel.

This combination is a contributing factor that leads to obesity, a major problem in the industry today. A recent CDC study states that 69 percent of long-haul drivers are obese compared to 31 percent of the national working population.

Obesity is a major health concern that can lead to high blood pressure, heart disease, type II diabetes, and sleep apnea. These diseases are preventable in many cases. The National Institute for Occupational Safety and Health (NIOSH) reports that 88 percent of all drivers had one of these conditions. Compounding the problems resulting from poor diet and exercise is the prevalence of smoking. NIOSH reports that approximately 54 percent of drivers' smoke.

Ask many drivers about body mass index (BMI) and they may tell you they do not give it much thought. BMI looks at a person's height and weight. While it only scratches the surface of an individual's overall health, it can indicate obesity and is now being looked at by the industry.

An adult with a BMI between 25 and 29.9 is considered overweight and someone with a BMI of 30 or higher is obese. A BMI equal to or greater than 40 would classify someone as morbidly obese.

The rate of morbid obesity in long-haul drivers, at 17 percent, is twice as high as the national working population, reports the CDC. In a study that looked at rookie drivers in their first two years on the road, drivers with a BMI higher than 35 had a 43 to 55 percent higher chance of having an accident when compared to drivers in the normal range. This indicates obesity could be a contributing factor to accidents.

Obesity is a contributing factor in the development of sleep apnea. This disorder can be related to obesity. Drivers that are at risk are required to undergo sleep tests to see if they have this disorder, and if so, they are required to use a CPAP machine while sleeping. This is an attempt to cut down on drowsy driving. A questionnaire conducted by law firm Pritzker Hageman administered at truck inspection stations in several U.S. states indicated that 28 percent of commercial drivers stated they had fallen asleep while driving at least once in the preceding month.

When looking at the current obesity epidemic among the truck driver population, it becomes clear that things need to change. The nature of the job, and the demands that the industry places on drivers, is costing companies money in addition to making our drivers sick. As drivers' fitness level decreases and their weight increases, many yield to the demands of the industry and leave the field in search of new work. What if this trend could be reversed and drivers could attain better personal fitness levels?

Many companies have started to put in fitness facilities at terminals. However, with the drivers constantly being on the go, many of these facilities sit unused. Unless they become part of an overall wellness program, these sites represent a waste of money.

A more effective, long-term solution is a wellness program that looks at the individual employee. Companies must make the employee's health the priority with fitness assessments, programs that are specific to everyone's goals, and constant monitoring.

Many drivers and regular employees for that matter feel unappreciated and overworked, so a financial commitment by companies that shows they care about the employee and his/her overall health will go a long way. The companies must look at this like any other process improvement project with better driver health as the goal.

The annual turnover rate in large truckload carriers hovers around 100 percent. When you take into consideration that it costs $3,000 to $5,000 to recruit and train one driver, it is costing the industry $3 billion to $5 billion annually to keep the one million or so driver positions filled, according to a recent Forbes article.

Instead of working to find replacements for our drivers, why not spend some money to make them healthy? What if the industry could add three to five years to a driver's career by helping them to attain a better personal level of fitness and overall health? This goal would make them more productive employees and lower driver attrition due to health issues related to obesity. In addition, a comprehensive individualized wellness program could make them safer drivers.

While healthcare costs continue to increase and companies scramble to find ways to make people more accountable for their own personal health, the approach to truck drivers must be different. We count on these individuals to deliver the things we often take for granted. If we cannot keep store shelves stocked and gas at the pumps, then what would happen? We must help keep our driver workforce healthy, or one day the store shelves may be bare.

It is your job to help your employees stay healthy. Encourage them to exercise when possible and do whatever it takes to help them accomplish their goals. An employee that is healthy is more productive and much happier.

CHAPTER SEVEN

Building a Winning Team.

-I hire people brighter than me and then I get out of their way.

-Lee Iacocca

As managers, the first thing that we need to realize is that we are only as good as the team we can assemble to do the work. If you go to the local bookstore, you can easily become overwhelmed by the number of books on management. The question is which method of management is correct? The answer could be swayed by what you need the team to do. From a supply chain perspective, I would like to render my opinion on how to select, lead and motivate a winning team.

Supply chain management is a complex environment and requires skilled personnel for the undertaking to be a success. If we look at the moving parts in a supply chain, then we can see why this is so important. Materials planning and inventory control require one set of skills on the inbound side. Transportation on the outbound side requires a different skill set. You will hear logistics people recite this motto. We need to get the *right* products, in the *right* place, in the *right* quantity and condition, at the *right* time. This can also be true when it comes to building your team. Building a team means you need the *right* people, in the *right* places, with the *right* skills. Knowing that is the case, how should a manager handle that situation? Personality is one of the most important things to look at when putting together the perfect team. Some people have instilled in them a sense of team, and some do not. Finding those individuals that can work as a unit is a key element.

If you need to find your team players, it is as easy as watching how people interact. During busy times, which employee is asking if others need help or is volunteering to take on more in their spare time. It always seems that the busiest people find ways to help, and that is usually because they have better time management skills. Sure, they could sit and do nothing, but instead they choose to help a teammate. This is a classic example of someone you would want to choose for your team. Sometimes the most talented individuals are not the best ones for your team. Knut Rockne, one of America's greatest coaches, once said, "The secret is to work less as individuals and more as a team. As a coach, I play not my eleven best, but my best eleven." That is the reason companies like to hire athletes or former military members. These individuals have been conditioned to work in a team environment. In their minds, reaching an objective or goal is what is important regardless of personal reward. Find a person with supply chain skills and a selfless sense of team, and you will have a real keeper. Let us assume you get all your team members. That is great, so how do you lead them?

I have seen an endless variety of management styles in my career. Some of them were good and some of them were bad. I have seen managers that have fantastic people skills and ones that this skill is virtually non-existent. Being able to assess talent is something that you will need to be able to do to be successful at building a great team.

"The best executive is the one who has sense enough to pick good men to do what he wants done, and self-restraint enough to keep from meddling with them while they do it." Theodore Roosevelt

At some point, the bird must leave the nest, so let people make decisions. As a leader, you must let the team members alone. If you have picked creative and team-oriented individuals, then the possibilities are limitless. The creativity of the unit is greater than that of one individual and unless you let loose of the reins, you will never know what the group could achieve.

If you have managed anyone more than ten minutes, then you know everyone is different. Some of your team members will be go-getters and waiting for that next opportunity, and some will be content to sit and do the job you have assigned them. One thing a leader will never forget is that you must treat each type of employee the same. Always assume that all your workers want to move up and treat them as a finite resource. Get them all the training available and cross train them when possible. If opportunities become available in the company, encourage them to apply if they are qualified. Never let a good employee leave to go to another company. If they do, then a leader should take that as a personal failure. It is difficult to find good employees and once they are trained and familiar with the corporate culture, you should help them along their career path. Remember, you can never be promoted until you have trained your replacement, so look at each team member in that way.

As a manager, you will be required to do the performance evaluations for each of your team members. When this annual event presents itself, be honest. No one ever got any better without constructive criticism. It is important to remember that it is not what you say, but how you say it. Always be positive and stress the importance of the team member to the unit. This time is also a great time to draw attention to areas that could require more training for this employee. An employee with a sense of team will take this as positive and want to become better.

Ask questions and pay attention to their reactions and, above all else, listen. As a leader, the best skill you can develop is listening. If one of your worker's performances has dropped, then listening may uncover the cause of this event.

Never forget we all have personal lives, and they intertwine with work. Make sure you know what is going on with your people and react accordingly. Do not be a manager that wants to be off for your family events and then expect your subordinate to miss theirs. Treat them as you would want to be treated.

As I have said before, leadership is a privilege and one that should not be taken lightly. It is a challenging job that requires all your efforts and energies but done correctly can provide a great sense of satisfaction. If you are a good leader, then it will not take long for the word to get around and when it does, you will see your career flourish.

Always try to promote from within, since this helps the company when you can retain and promote good employees. Constantly going outside the company for new managers only serves to undermine the current staff. Sure, there are times when new blood is needed, but, when at all possible, reward your people with a good career path.

As companies struggle to fill vital supply chain roles, it will become more important to recruit, train and build a valuable team environment. It is not an easy task and requires leaders with unique people skills. While it is challenging to build a successful team, I cannot think of anything that is more rewarding than a team reaching a goal. So, look at your current managers and think to yourself, which ones are leaders. Are there managers who aren't quite there? Perhaps additional mentoring or training is needed. This may require a long hard look at your staff and some tough changes, but the alternative is worse. When you start seeing drops in efficiency, employee turnover and low morale, then the damage is done. If you want your company to thrive, then you must find your leaders and let them lead.

Get your stars the additional training so they can reach their full potential. Be the helpful manager and recognize and help those who need you. I think the biggest compliment that I ever received was when my boss told me I was a Level Five Leader. Of course, he was referring to the Jim Collins book, "Good to Great." I did not really know what he meant until I got a copy of the book myself.

"The level 5 leader was the triumph of humility and fierce resolve. How a level 5 leader manifests humility? They routinely credit others, external factors, and good luck for the company success, but when results are poor, they blame themselves. They also act quietly, calmly, and determinedly relying on inspired standards not inspiring charisma to motivate. Level 5 leadership unwavering will utterly be intolerant of mediocrity. They are stoic in their resolve to do whatever it takes to produce great results terminating everything else and they select superb successors wanting their companies to become even more successful in the future." (Collins, 30)

Major Winters, the commander of Easy Company that was nominated for the Medal of Honor for his actions on D-Day, has a great list of things that are needed to be a leader. He called them, "Leadership at the point of a bayonet." (2)

1. Strive to be a leader of character competence and courage.

2. Lead from the front. Say, "Follow me!" and then lead the way.

3. Stay in top physical shape—physical stamina is the root of mental toughness.

4. Develop your team. If you know your people, are fair and set realistic goals and expectations, and lead by example, you will develop teamwork.

5. Delegate responsibility to your subordinates and let them do their job. You can't do a good job if you don't have a chance to use your imagination and creativity.

6. Anticipate problems and prepare to overcome obstacles. Don't wait until you get to the top of the ridge and then make up your mind.

7. Remain humble. Don't worry about who receives the credit. Never let power or authority go to your head.

8. Take a moment of self-reflection. Look at yourself in the mirror every night and ask yourself if you did your best.

9. True satisfaction comes from getting the job done. The key to a successful leader is to earn respect— not because of rank or position, but because you're a leader of character.

10. Hang tough! Never, ever, give up.

CHAPTER EIGHT

Process Improvement to Grow Your Business.

-Perfection is not attainable. But if we can chase perfection, we can catch excellence.

-Vince Lombardi

For over twenty-five years, I was involved in logistics and transportation, with the last sixteen of those years being spent with a large apparel corporation in their private fleet. During those sixteen years, I cannot remember a single year where the private fleet did not have to defend its very existence. Each year, the argument seemed to escalate until the cost reductions started. At that time, the corporate answer to cutting costs fell to cutting head count, but I have always felt that cutting headcount may impact the customer experience. In my mind, saving money meant saving my co-worker's jobs and so I voluntarily became involved to save the fleet by using process improvement.

All of us can agree that the world is changing, and process improvement has become more important than ever. As many companies are closing their doors and others are struggling to stay afloat, it has become imperative to find ways to save money and attaining greater efficiency may shine some light on a seemingly dark business operating environment. It can be an overwhelming feeling of helplessness as you watch your department or company fail. This feeling is shared by many transportation professionals, especially now. For many business owners, the situation has turned from operating to merely surviving, and everyone is scrambling for solutions.

Author George Eckes said, *"Six Sigma, at its basic level, is attempting to improve both effectiveness and efficiency at the same time."* (Eckes, 2003) The key is reducing variation, which will yield a more consistent process, and, in my opinion, our smaller operation could benefit from process improvement. We did not have the assets to spend on large groups of trained process improvement people, but we did have a small handful of folks in our department with many years of industry experience and it would have to be up to us to fight to keep our department going. Using a five-step process, we started by looking for opportunities.

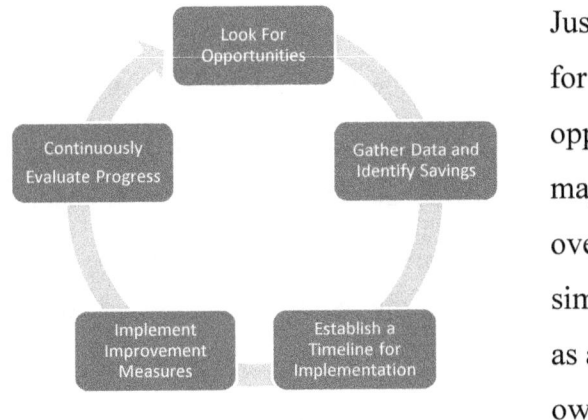

Just looking for opportunities may sound overly simplistic, but as a business owner, you must be able to take a hard look at your current situation and question what you do and do not do well. *"A fundamental tool of the Lean journey is a baseline analysis. The flyby objective of this powerful tool is to define the current state of a chosen business process, evaluate the system for waste and opportunity, create a (future) proposed state of the process, and formulate a plan of action to get there."* (Hoerl, 2003) Sometimes that first look inside your own performance can be difficult. At first, many people were resistant to the process and others had no interest at all. Perhaps, they felt that saying things needed to be improved only implied that they had failed, but that was not the case at all. Every company has room for improvement and the key is finding where to focus your attention.

You see, it is not about mastering a complex methodology, but rather about taking the simplest aspects of basic business process improvement and combining it with today's high-powered products. By doing this, any business, large or small, can benefit from process improvement. One thing that is imperative is that you must be a creative thinker. You must force yourself to look at problems from every angle and play the childhood game of **what does not belong** as it relates to your operations. When you are looking for opportunities in step one, you must ask yourself whether this opportunity can generate the desired savings that the department needs. So, whether you are looking to save a hundred thousand dollars a year or one million, the project you choose must have the ability to meet the goal or you need to keep looking. To do this, one could use a process map. Lean Six Sigma Logistics summed it up. *"Waste happens! Once we face this brutal fact, we can eliminate it."* (Martichenko, 2005) Being able to identify the waste is where many people fail and that is why Six Sigma training can be so helpful.

The first improvement project was presented to me when my boss proposed this question. "We are spending a bunch of money on ocean container detention and demurrage. Do you think you could reduce that?"

The second improvement project started when my boss called me in to his office and told me to find a way to cut the cost of outside fuel purchases for the fleet by a nickel a gallon. He gave me one day to come up with a plan to present to the Vice President of Supply Chain for approval.

The third project was started when our corporate office ordered us to cut costs by $200,000. The projects selected were determined to be the following:

- Project One – Reduce the annual detention and demurrage container expense.
- Project Two – Reduce the cost associated with outside fuel for the private fleet.
- Project Three – Increase tractor utilization and reduce driver delay.

The next step was to see just where we stood and gather the necessary data. As with any process improvement methodology, one must gather the data. Looking at the detention and demurrage numbers for the previous year was shocking. The department was expensing well over $300,000 annually.

The second project was very rushed since I was only given one day to prepare. My first stop was the fuel clerk. After a quick discussion, she pulled all the fuel invoices for the past six months. Just talking with her and getting her input was vital to the success of the project. Once all the information on fuel purchases for our department was gathered, it was a matter of identifying variations in the fuel purchasing habits of our drivers.

In the meantime, our department held a meeting and our boss told us that corporate had instructed him to find a way to save $200,000 that year. As my co-workers talked about turning off lights and other ways to conserve money, it became apparent that to reach the goal; the solution had to be hidden in our processes. After a quick discussion with management, it was obvious that no one knew the tractor utilization for the fleet. My attention quickly turned to that analysis to see if increased fleet utilization could increase efficiency.

For the first project, the goal was a 10% annual savings. The current process had been in place for years and dealing with the fleet, dispatch, distribution centers and steamship lines to change their current habits and mindset would be a challenge. Since this was uncharted territory, the goal was set lower, knowing it could always be revised.

The information for the second project was analyzed quickly. After reviewing the driver fueling data, there was one specific chain that had consistently displayed lower fuel prices. The driver manager would be required to work with the drivers to have them fuel at the selected locations. The second part of the process would require that drivers make better use of bulk fuel facilities. The Vice President was happy when we told him we estimated that the department could save fifteen cents per gallon on outside fuel using this plan. Since this was ten cents better than the directive, the Vice President approved the plan. Later that day, with help from the fuel clerk and driver manager, we decided to fix the fuel problem and instituted our program.

While reviewing my calculations for the third project, it became apparent that our utilization was much lower than expected due to increased waiting times at the ports and borders. After calculating the savings that could be realized by increasing utilization, it was obvious that we could meet the goal, not by cutting cost, but my improving our efficiency. In other words, we would have to squeeze all the efficiency we could out of each tractor to reach the goal of $200,000. The department started right away trying to reduce the amount of delay at ports and borders by utilizing better scheduling and dispatch procedures.

Each project was given top priority and was implemented immediately. The length of each project hinged on meeting the required goal. Each project could impact the overall daily operations over the long term and, therefore, it was imperative to leave the timeline open.

For the first project, the company was maintaining a database of these containers manually, and it was a jumbled mess. When a container was picked up at the port, it was entered in the system. Containers picked up empty were allowed seven days of free time and those picked up loaded were allowed twenty-seven days. What would make the process more efficient and, therefore, yield the results needed? Then, the simple answer presented itself. Improving the tracking system was the focus. The programmer that built the system was asked to install a color-coding system. These colors would alert everyone in the department to a late container. After much discussion, he changed the system, but he made sure to comment that there would never be a day where a container was not late. The hardest part of the process was dealing with distribution centers to help them understand that turning in these containers on time and not letting them sit on their yards was beneficial to the company. In the past, the containers would be used as storage at their facilities and these charges were passed to our department, but the company was still bearing this cost. It became imperative that all the DC managers felt involved in the process and, by doing that, we never had any problems getting trailers unloaded and taken back to the ports. Dispatch was updated on the new system before the project went live.

Project two took shape quickly and with the help of the fuel clerk and driver manager, we put our plan in motion. Each week, we would post maps with the lowest fuel along routes and send messages to drivers, letting them know where the cheapest fuel could be found. Eventually, some drivers added the truck stop app to their phones to see fuel prices in real time.

Project three was also quick as we measured current delay and utilization and then worked with operations to reduce it by utilizing better scheduling and dispatch procedures. We would send trucks southbound to ports and borders only when we had cleared northbound loads to match up with them. Since we had a few extra days built into the system on the southbound side, we did not have any delay issues and as the goods cleared customs at the borders, we would dispatch a truck immediately to head that way.

When you take a process and improve it, that process must be continually improved and monitored to make sure that it meets or exceeds the analyzed outcome. Being able to sustain any realized gains is a key aspect of the process. "At the tactical level it sustains the gains of individual projects, and at the strategic level it broadens the gains of the Six Sigma initiative overall." (Trudell, 2006) These projects were part of a greater savings initiative. Because of that fact, they required constant monitoring and refining. Each of these projects was managed and constantly improved. In that way, constant savings could be seen and communicated to the fleet. Allowing people to see that the projects were having an impact on operational savings was at the heart of their success.

For project one, the savings started immediately. The first year, we cut the cost of detention and demurrage by $100,000. By the second year, we saw the first day of no late containers. In five years, we cut the annual cost for the department by 86%. By adding color coding, we were able to have better visibility of containers that needed to be re-routed to ports and that one simple change saved a great deal of money.

Project two saw results much higher than expected as well. The initial goal was a savings on outside fuel of fifteen cents a gallon. The plan we put into place was measured for one year and yielded an estimated savings of thirty-five cents a gallon, which translated to an overall estimated savings of $275,000.

Project three had a goal of saving $200,000 within a year. It only took several weeks for us to see utilization jump to almost 100%. Within four months, the project had reduced driver delay by 3,400 hours and it was estimated that the project would exceed the expected annual savings goal.

These projects beat the goals set by management with only a limited departmental budget, and without the luxury of hiring vast numbers of dedicated process improvement people to study the operation for months. Process improvement does not have to be overly complicated. If you can use Excel or some other form of spreadsheet to organize and manipulate your numbers, you can take those first exciting steps to improving operations.

In conclusion, you must know where you are; where you want to go; and then determine a way to get there. If you understand your business and have some creativity, there will always be ways to improve processes and find ways to save money. During these difficult times, we can all benefit from becoming students of process improvement systems. Too many people give up and say it cannot be done.

As a leader, you must make tough decisions. These decisions could impact the company your own or at which you work. Cutting costs and reducing variation in processes can go a long way into improving your bottom line. The hardest part of any project is getting people to buy into it. You must find ways to get people involved and always tout the importance of cost reductions. Don't fall for that adage, "This is the way it has always been done."

There will always be ways to reduce waste in many areas and in my opinion, many companies really don't have any idea how much money they could be saving. Teach your people to be process improvement minded and always strive to cut costs. Do that, and your company will reap the benefits.

CHAPTER NINE

It Is Just a Job!

-Never get so busy making a living that you forget to make a life.

-Dolly Parton

When I was working at a large corporation, one day an old man of about eighty years of age walked into my boss's empty office and sat down. He just sat there in silence. I glanced in the office of one of my co-workers and asked him about the lonely man. My co-worker said that was Mr. Thomas, and that he had worked there for forty years managing the operations and building the business before he retired. Since that was before I was hired, I was curious and wanted to know more. After some investigation, I learned that he was quite the dynamic leader and worked harder than anyone. His driving ambition had paved the way for the state of the current operation, but in the process, he failed to take time to have a family, or as far as I know, even get married. His whole life had been working and now he was a forgotten man. Apparently, his only friend was my boss that used to work for him. So, he would come up several times a week and just sit in his office. After learning this, it changed the way I looked at work. Up to this point, I was on the path to becoming Mr. Thomas. I had always wanted to accomplish so much; I guess I was thinking somehow that would make me a little more important in the eyes of others. Like Mr. Thomas, I had placed everything else on the back burner, thinking there would always be time to do those things after I'd accomplished my goals. The sad fact I soon realized is that day would never come. It was not long after that I started to make sure I took all my vacation and personal days.

I would often see that tendency to overwork in new managers. Practically overnight, their egos would take over and they would be obsessed with work. I understand that when someone gets a promotion; it is an important achievement in their life, but it is simply their transition from individual contributor to something more. Some new managers suddenly become tyrants, standing, and barking orders, driving employees through fear and intimidation, expecting subordinates to give every ounce of their energy to the success of the company. Other new managers work longer and longer hours and push aside family obligations. The trick is to work smarter and not longer. Time management skills become even more important as you move up. If you see this happening, you should sit down and have a serious conversation with your manager. If that person, is you, then you need to take a long look in the mirror and have a conversation with yourself. My father had a great saying, "The graveyards are full of people that thought they couldn't be replaced." When he would say that when I was young, I would always smile. Despite his dedication and sacrifice, our company was running long after Mr. Thomas took his retirement. No one is indispensable, so never place work above family or personal health.

When I was a manager in the restaurant industry, the pace was grueling, to say the least. The restaurant industry is extremely high stress, and I could tell that the stress of the situation was wearing on one of my fellow managers. He was pushing himself entirely too hard, so I sat down to put things in a way he could understand. I told him to imagine having a point of view from over the restaurant. Now, pull back till your point of view is over the town, then over the state, then over the country and finally over the world. I told him we run a tiny restaurant in a little town in Virginia and if you drop over dead, the regional supervisor will just tell me to run the store and sadly nobody would care. He started to calm down as he realized his demise would not garner much fanfare. Suddenly, his chest pains faded, and he was back to work. I think he needed to see things from a different point of view and understand that it was just a job and not worth getting so stressed out about.

Later, when I was working in the transportation industry, I had a good friend who had been with the company for twenty-three years. Due to the introduction of a new supervisor, he decided he was going to retire or leave the company. I can remember going to his office and sitting down with him, trying to talk him into staying.

My friend oversaw the backhaul division for our private fleet and was a key person in our department. When you handle backhauls in a transportation fleet, you impact profitability greatly, and this gentleman had made the organization more efficient and much more profitable during the past few years. I asked him if he could try and stay just two more years to make it to his twenty-five-year milestone. He stopped typing away on his computer and looked at me and said, "Do you think on your deathbed you will say, 'Gee I wish I'd just worked a little harder for this company?'" I found the statement almost comical and chuckled, but since I knew this gentleman's sense of humor, I could tell he was dead serious. For me, that question put into perspective how he framed his decision to leave. He looked at it as life-or-death. He did not want to stay there one more minute, much less two years. He was so adamant about not working for this new supervisor that he was willing to throw away the twenty-three years of seniority he had built up. To him, it was a matter of principle and I admired him for his decision. What did the departure of that key player cost the company?

That brings up the question: why do people leave? Is it because of the work? In this instance, probably not since this gentleman had been there so long. It was clearly the new boss and I want to provide some back story to help you understand the situation.

For the previous three years, our department had struggled to stay afloat. Corporate wanted to outsource the transportation department, and that was something that many companies were doing at the time. I've always been of the mindset that if a decision is the right one for the company, then I have no problem getting behind it. But to make that decision, the numbers must support it.

There was a group of individuals in our department that were part of the team to study the justification of the private fleet. My friend was one of those key people and I had become part of that process totally by accident.

One day several months before, I was busy moving freight internationally, when I had heard rumors, they wanted us to justify fleet operations yet again. On the way to the copy room, I passed my boss's office. He looked to be extremely stressed out and so I ducked my head in and in passing said, "I know you're trying to do this project and I may be able to help you with it. I have a master's degree in logistics, and I used to study these kinds of things." Since he had no idea of my academic background, he glanced up at me with a sort of bewildered look and said, "Yeah, you take a look at it and let me know what you think."

I really didn't think much about it, but I did go home and start working on a plan to better utilize the fleet and save the company money. I knew that our fleet was only moving a percentage of our companies' total freight, so I started looking at all the companies' available lanes. It turned out that many of the lanes were being given away at higher rates to carriers. My overall objective was to right size the fleet, increase utilization and increase profits by eliminating loads that were inefficient.

My mindset has always been to look at the totality of the company freight as a network of lanes and then simply make the best use of lanes that help the fleet reach maximum efficiency. Our fleet could run many of the giveaway lanes at a lower cost. The rest of the loads could be outsourced. When I did things in that way, it became apparent that the company was not utilizing their fleet to its highest potential. When I completed my study, I estimated we could save about one to two million a year for the company, but it would require the corporate supply chain people to allow us to select the lanes that we wanted to run.

I was sitting at home on a Saturday at my computer when my boss called me. He asked me if I had been working on this project and wanted to know if I had figured anything out. I forwarded him my analysis while we were on the phone. He was silent for a moment before he said, "This is brilliant!"

I didn't think it was brilliant; it was just looking at it from a different angle. This study and another one I worked on resulted in the corporate supply chain folks keeping the fleet for another year, but now the very people vowing to eliminate the fleet would be in charge from the corporate office. It was a bittersweet victory and upon the announcement; it had me looking for another job. I now understood the point my friend was making about his early retirement.

The point I'm trying to make is that a job is just a job, and you must keep in perspective that if you leave, somebody else will take your place. When I got to the point that corporate neither appreciated nor shared our vision of how to make the department the most efficient it could be, I moved on.

Just remember, if you become the best at your chosen profession, there will always be people looking to hire you. It is their loss, not yours, so you can't spend your day beating yourself up over the decision to move on. Always look at this as an opportunity to help some other company or start your own thing. Do what is best for you and your family.

Companies that continuously lose employees and have high turnover rates need to take a deeper look into why these people leave. It is a failure of the company to understand the needs of the employee and to balance those needs with the needs of the company to reach optimum efficiency.

Turnover rates are skyrocketing at businesses and help wanted signs adorn many windows throughout the country. How can this be fixed? The answer is simple. Leaders need to get better at what they do. They must get better at communicating and understanding the needs of the employees. An understanding leader will strive to find a way to balance work and life from the perspective of their employees. All people really want is to do their job, be paid well, and basically left alone.

As many corporations' struggle to find workers, often recruiters overlook many people that could be a fit as they search for the perfect candidate. Human resources recruiters do a great disservice in my opinion to the older workers and workers they feel don't specifically fit a role at a company. When looking for a key person, look beyond the printed resume at the person behind it. Many jobs are left unfilled simply because some folks are looking for that perfect employee. It is like the person that never gets married in fear that someone better will come along. How many great opportunities did they pass up waiting for the perfect one?

As a leader, it is important to find, hire, train and manage that employee. Things will never be easy on the road to becoming a great leader, but remember, at the end of the day, it is just a job. Strive to find a work life balance that works for you and helps your employees understand that as well. Being able to do that will make work much more fun and rewarding.

CHAPTER TEN

The Power of Positive Thinking.

-To be an overachiever, you must be an over-believer.

-Dabo Swinney

If you are given a task at work that seems impossible, then just take a minute to remember the events of one of the most significant days in history. I wanted to take a minute to look at the role of logistics on June 6th, 1944. When many of us think of this historic event, it conjures up the image of brave soldiers climbing into their landing crafts to end the war in Europe. What many people don't realize is that the invasion took over two years of planning. The allied forces knew the invasion would not be an easy one, since the Germans had placed one hundred- and fifty-thousand-gun emplacements along the twenty-four hundred mile stretch of coastline called the Atlantic Wall. The German General Erwin Rommel had also orchestrated a series of deadly obstacles along the beaches to slow or deter landing craft. He accomplished this by placing over thirty thousand stakes the size of telephone poles in the beach sand, along with over ten thousand large obstacles. These obstacles required the landing to take place at low tide, which resulted in the soldiers having to cross a three-hundred-yard stretch of beach with no cover. This stretch of beach became a killing field that was in range of one hundred twenty rifles, machine guns and artillery pieces.

The success of this operation would not have been possible without logistics. In the days before computers, a giant armada of over two thousand ships was loaded and readied to go. Each one with certain cargo that was loaded in a specific order. Each soldier landing on D-Day required a kit with ninety-six rounds of ammunition, six lbs. of food and twenty pints of water. Every two weeks, this kit would have to be replaced and every two hundred days, this specific soldier would need to be replaced with a fresh replacement. For each yard, a soldier moved he would require eighteen support personnel which included clerks, cooks, medics, and mechanics to help him accomplish his mission.

When you think of the amount of planning, it can become overwhelming. Then there was another issue. There were no docks for the ships to offload all these supplies to keep the troops moving forward. With no docks in allied hands, they had to bring the docks with them. Fifty-one giant concrete sections called floating Mulberry Harbours were constructed and sailed eighty miles to Normandy. These sections were connected, and compartments were flooded to sink them in place, creating a dock to off load supplies. These sections took six months to build and required sixty thousand tons of steel. The dock was placed at Omaha Beach and accommodated enough ships to move one truckload of supplies each minute.

To this day, it is hard to imagine how young men stepped off those boats and waded into the withering face of enemy fire, but they did. Some units suffered ninety-two percent casualties and along those beaches, over twenty-four hundred American soldiers would be killed on that day. We owe a debt of gratitude to all the men and women that participated in WWII and this historic invasion. The price of freedom is not free, and these people sacrificed for all of us.

Do you think these brave men and women had doubts as to the success of the mission? Maybe they did, but they had to focus on accomplishing what they needed to do and put all thought of failure out of their minds. If you let yourself think you may fail, then it becomes possible. Eliminate those thoughts and you cannot lose. By keeping those thoughts of failure in check, you can develop confidence. What does confidence have to do with leadership?

Confidence can be an issue for a new manager. Not unlike any other relationship, there is a time when the manager and subordinate are getting to know each other. The manager is assessing the strength and weaknesses of the worker and the worker is doing the same. Many managers never think about it, but just as I was told by the coach, there are eyes on you all the time. With this being the case, it is not unusual for a new manager to have confidence issues. Probably the best book ever written on this subject is *The Power of Positive Thinking.* I recommend that each new manager read this book since it contains so many things that are helpful.

If you can focus on winning instead of losing; victory instead of defeat, then your perspective can change. Have you ever met someone that is constantly negative? It always seems like that poor person has one bad break after another but stay positive and your future can change for the better. If you allow negative thoughts to creep into your day, they can overwhelm you. One of the best exercises from the book is to repeat the following affirmation each day ten times. "I can do all things through Christ which strengtheneth me." (Philippians 4:13). It is amazing the power of this exercise and how it can help your mind stay clear and focused on being successful.

In business, positive thinking plays a key role in success. By being positive, you can come up with a solution to any problem. At one point in my career, I was managing the movement of goods from the United States to the Yucatan area of Mexico. We supplied this manufacturing division by utilizing a third-party logistics company based in the US. This company would pull the equipment that we had spotted at various vendors across the Southeastern United States. I'd done that for about a year when Hurricane Katrina bore down on the Port of New Orleans. Of course, we all know the damage that Hurricane Katrina did to the city of New Orleans, but overnight it basically wiped out the seven trucking companies that the third-party logistics company was using to move our goods all over the Southeast and the port was closed for operations.

I can remember the meeting the day after the storm hit when my boss was on the phone with supply chain at our corporate office. As we all sat huddled around the phone, my boss told everyone that we would have to shut down the manufacturing at the Yucatan plant due to lack of supply and the situation with the third-party logistics company.

I have always been a very positive person and I don't believe that there's any situation in which there is not a solution. As my father always used to say, "When somebody says something can't be done there's already somebody out there doing it." I spoke up stating that we had trailers spotted at our vendors, and we still had a private fleet to utilize, so we could fix it. We simply had to stage the goods that we needed at the vendors and load them on the available trailers. I then contacted the steamship line and asked them where the nearest available port was located. The Port of Panama City, FL was the closest, so they docked there, and our private fleet picked up the trailers at the vendors. We sailed them on time and the factory remained open.

I believe the reason that operation was successful was that I did not let the defeated thoughts creep into my head. I knew there had to be a way to fix this situation and our group was able to get it done.

Remember that success is what you make it. You will have people that doubt you. Zig Zigler, one of the world's most successful authors, made it clear in his book, *See You at The Top.* "One point you need to clearly understand is that education and intelligence are not the same thing." Never let people tell you that you cannot do something. If you believe in yourself and have faith, then anything is possible."

The biggest thing a new manager must do is believe in themselves and have confidence and faith in their abilities. There will always be those people that try to hold you back or put you down, but you can't let those people get inside your head. If you have the mindset that you want to be a leader of integrity, humility, character, and conviction, then you can change the world.

"The greatest secret for eliminating the inferiority complex, which is another term for deep and profound self-doubt, is to fill your mind to overflowing with faith. Develop a tremendous faith in God and that will give you a humble yet realistic faith in yourself." (Peale 60)

If you find yourself lacking the confidence to do the job, then maybe you have to ask yourself, why am I doing this? Is it for the money? Is it for the recognition? Or is it because you want to impact, and often times, profoundly change the lives of the people that you lead? If you answered yes to the last question, then I believe there's no doubt that you will be an exceptional leader, because leadership is about service.

In those years I spent in the trucking industry, I watched people treat truck drivers as second-class citizens. I looked at managing those individuals as a tremendous honor. It was my job to make sure they had whatever they needed to get the job done. Those drivers were the hardest working people I ever met.

As a new manager, you will need to develop a sense of humility and service towards the people that work for you. Put yourself in their shoes and understand that they are counting on you for assistance to do their jobs. This world is a small place and we need to take care of each other. At the time I wrote this book, I had not opened my father's copy of *The Power of Positive Thinking* for many years. He had given me the book when I was a child. It had been many years since his passing and the binding was torn and the pages yellowed. Buried deep within the pages was a folded article from Reader's Digest Magazine. The sides of the article were tattered and worn. At first, I thought it was a bookmark, then I realized my father had tucked it away in the book, so it must have had significance to him. The article was about self discipline and I wanted to share part of that with you.

"It is indeed this capacity to discipline ourselves that is the root of all virtues and the fount of all freedom. To be morally free man must muster his instincts. He must in the words of the scripture rule his own spirit. If only we could realize that character cannot be built nor anything of value ever accomplished without self discipline." (Cronin 54-55)

As you move forward in your careers, always remember to have a positive attitude and strive to be a supportive leader. Someone once told me that it does not matter what job title you end up having or how much money you make. What people will remember is how you treated them and how you made them feel. If you do this, you will not only be remembered as a good leader, but most of all as a good person. Lead with integrity and character, but most of all, enjoy this time in your business career. You have the chance to impact the lives of others. You have the unique opportunity to lead, and that is what this journey is all about.

References

Collins, J. (2001). *Good to Great*. New York: Harper Collins Publishing.

Cronin. (1956). Unless You Deny Yourself. *Readers Digest*, pp. 54-55.

Donnithorne, C. L. (1994). *The West Point Way of Leadership*. New York: Doubleday.

DuVernay, C. B. (2008). Micromanage at Your Peril. *Harvard Management Update*.

Eckes, G. (2003). *Six Sigma for Everyone*. Hoboken, NJ: John Wiley & Sons, Inc.

Finkelstein, S. (2018). The Best Leaders are Great Teachers. *Harvard Business Review*.

Hoerl, R. D. (2003). *Leading Six Sigma*. New York, NY: Prentice Hall.

Keller, G. (2013). *The One Thing*. Austin: Bard Publishing.

Langlois, C. (2018). Major Winters Rules of Leadership. *Calibre Press*.

Martichenko, D. T. (2005). *Lean Six Sigma Logistics Strategic Development to Operational Success*. Boca Raton, FL: J. Ross Publishing.

Miech, C. (2020). The Negative Effects of Micromanagement and What it Says to Your Employees. *Blog*.

Peale. (1952). *The Power of Positive Thinking*. Englewood Cliffs: Prentice Hall.

Peale. (1954). *A Guide to Confident Living*. New York: Prentice Hall.

Robbins, A. (n.d.). *Unlimited Power*. New York: Ballentine Books.

Thomas, W. B. (2002). Crucibles of Leadership. *Harvard Business Review.*

Trudell, B. C. (2006). *Lean Six Sigma That Works.* New York, NY: AMACOM.

Valcour, M. (2020). Anyone Can Learn to Be a Better Leader. *Harvard Business Review.*

Zig Zigler. (1974). *See You At The Top.* Carrolton, Texas: Pelican Publishing.

www.ingramcontent.com/pod-product-compliance
Lightning Source LLC
Chambersburg PA
CBHW051543170526
45165CB00002B/866